The Language of Old Brick and Mortar

The bricks gossip softly, a clink and a clack,
Trading tales of the neighbors they lack.
They roll their eyes at the echoing whack,
Of toddlers in sneakers who never look back.

The wallpaper chuckles at stains from the past,
Each splash of the juice, a memory cast.
It winks at the children, growing up fast,
As dance parties happen, shadows are amassed.

Murmurs of Memory in the Air

The ceiling fan spins with a comical joke,
As the light flickers on, it's laughter they stoke.
They reminisce about the pie that they broke,
While the old clock ticks, preserving the poke.

The curtains giggle at the sun's warm embrace,
Pulling cheeks in a mock, joyous race.
And the mouse in the corner just wishes for space,
To join in the fun, oh what a strange place!

Echoing Footfalls of the Past

Steps of the funny, the awkward and shy,
Tap dance on floors with a giggling sigh.
Here comes the cat, with a leap to the sky,
While the dog snorts a laugh, oh my, oh my!

The memories clatter beneath winter's bright glow,
As the laughter of children is carried below.
They bounce down the stairs, a jubilant show,
Turning echoes to music, a timeless tableau.

Unheard Stories in the Gloom

In the shadows, secrets creep,
A rubber chicken's laugh runs deep.
Noses wrinkled, cats will stare,
While mice plot mischief, unaware.

Dusty corners hide some jest,
A sock puppet claims it's the best.
Every creak reveals the fun,
As lonely ghosts begin to run.

Reflections of Distant Echoes

Chairs creak like they know a joke,
The ancient clock starts to poke.
Ghostly giggles fill the air,
Echoed sneezes, who knows where?

With every tick, a story spins,
From jokers lost, to playful wins.
A ghostly wink, a laugh so sly,
In this quiet, silliness flies.

The Heartbeat of Abandoned Places

In silence, laughter finds a home,
A wayward cat makes shadows roam.
The dusty floorboards start to sway,
While echoes of good times come to play.

Paint peels back, revealing glee,
A whirlwind of ghosts, a quirky spree.
Each step brings giggles, a charming sound,
As silly antics in stillness abound.

Subtle Sounds of Elysium

A choir of crickets, off-key tunes,
Dancing with the fickle moons.
Laughter trickles through the light,
As merry hoots take flight at night.

With dusty beams of sunshine bright,
Cartwheeling humor feels just right.
In cracks and crevices, glee ignites,
A playful spirit that ignites delights.

Shadows Speak Softly

In the corners, shadows play,
They giggle softly, night and day.
In a hurry, they trip and score,
Who knew they'd dance behind the door?

A lamp flickers, they jump with glee,
Invisible friends, just you and me.
With winks and nudges, they plot and tease,
As they cause a ruckus with playful ease.

Listen closely, a tickle in the air,
As shadows joke without a care.
Their antics bold, a comical sight,
In the silent corners, full of delight.

The Language of Stone

Granite giggles, marble's mirth,
In stony laughter, they find their worth.
A pebble chats with a statue tall,
With earthen humor that covers all.

Rocks whisper secrets in a funny tone,
About the days when they stood alone.
They poke and prod, with cracks and chips,
Sharing tales through shaky quips.

Jokes carved deeply in every seam,
Living stone holds more than a dream.
When you lean in close, chuckles abound,
In the silent hush, there's laughter found.

Hushed Tales of the Past

Old herbs and spices, a tale to tell,
In the spice rack, they promise to dwell.
With each jar, a chuckle or sneeze,
As they plot mischief with silly tease.

Dusty books, their spines all cracked,
In quiet corners, their humor's stacked.
Page by page, they share a laugh,
In their musty realm, a quirky gaffe.

Pictures on the wall grin wide and bright,
In hues of laughter, they spark delight.
Tales of yesteryear, with a wink and grin,
In the hushed atmosphere, the fun begins.

Unseen Conversations

Behind every picture, a giggle hides,
With tales of old, where joy abides.
Each frame a portal to laughter's stream,
Where unseen friends plot the next great scheme.

Chairs creak softly, a playful debate,
As single socks share their dating fate.
In the leg of a table, a ticklish sigh,
With a bump and a thud, they wave goodbye.

In corners where cobwebs spin like lace,
The dust bunnies join the merry chase.
Their chatter erupting in fits of cheer,
In a world unseen, where fun is near.

Lurking Harmonies

In the corner, a giggle hides,
Dancing shadows on the slides.
Beneath the table, chuckles soar,
An old cat plotting, oh, what a bore!

Taps of tiny feet in the night,
Echoes of glee, a playful fright.
Socks on the ceiling, where did they flee?
An unseen ballet, come look and see!

Lost Harmonies of Rooms

In the kitchen, pots start to clink,
As if they're chatting, don't you think?
The fridge hums tunes of old rock and roll,
While the stove tries to take center pole.

A broom does a tango, all on its own,
Mopping the floor, it just won't moan.
A spatula winks, it's quite the sight,
In this quirky kitchen, there's pure delight!

The Muted Echo

In the hallway, a secret plots,
The old clock ticks in funny spots.
Every tick is like a tease,
Tickling ears, a merry breeze!

Books on shelves hold gags untold,
With stories of mischief and legends bold.
An echo of laughter spills from the past,
In this quiet house, good times amassed!

Shadows of Unspoken Words

Underneath the couch, a sneeze is heard,
A dusty tale, an unintelligible word.
The coffee table's dressed up in dust,
But it knows secrets, oh, it must!

A mirror grins, reflecting tales,
Of cozy nights and wild emails.
Behind the curtains, giggles flare,
In this fun house, joy's everywhere!

Shimmering Silences

In a room where secrets laugh,
Laughter dances with the draft.
Socks are hiding all alone,
While the cat claims every throne.

Chairs creak with a jolly sound,
As the dust bunnies gather 'round.
A ticklish tick is simply sly,
Tickling the clock that winks goodbye.

A fridge hums a playful tune,
While spoons groove beneath the moon.
The walls lean in with glee and cheer,
As the plants conspire, never fear.

In the corners, shadows play,
Replaying jokes from yesterday.
And an old book, slightly torn,
Chortles softly, never worn.

The Soft Tread of Time

Time tiptoes with a grin and a jig,
Bouncing back like a bright red fig.
Tick-tock laughter, what a sight,
Running races with the night.

Old shoes keep a gentle beat,
As the carpet hums, oh so sweet.
Dust motes prance like tiny fairies,
In the spaces of bright cherries.

Muffins giggle in the tin,
As the clock spins wide on a whim.
Willy-nilly, the moments fly,
Twirling round like cake in a pie.

Echoes bounce off every door,
Hugging stories from the floor.
With every step, it seems to tease,
Happily caught in a mind's breeze.

Currents of Stillness

Stillness flows like syrup thick,
A river waits for a silly trick.
Puddles smile at clouds above,
While the sun plays coy, like a dove.

The sofa sighs, old springs complain,
As cushions plot a bouncy campaign.
Laughing pillows, bright and bold,
Share recipes for dreams untold.

Lamps flicker a friendly jest,
Challenging shadows to a quest.
Each corner snug with muffs of light,
Keeps the giggles tucked in tight.

Books on shelves whisper a wink,
Telling tales where walls can't blink.
Silence fills the room with cheer,
As absurdity blooms, my dear.

Fragments of Faded Echoes

Echoes float like floating bread,
Stale but funny, that's what they said.
Secrets bounce in the hallway clear,
Tickled pink by a ghostly cheer.

Old photos wink with a silly face,
Captured moments, a timeless grace.
Smiles tucked in crinkled frames,
Chuckle softly, no need for names.

The attic grins in dusty glee,
As echoes sing of giddy spree.
Furniture sways to a tune of yore,
While the curtains giggle on the floor.

Slowly fading, yet brand-new,
Tales that only walls once knew.
And as laughter leaks through the seams,
Life feels lighter with its dreams.

Eavesdropping on Silence

In corners where giggles hide,
The cat rolls over, full of pride.
It hears the shadows talk and tease,
While dust bunnies dance with the breeze.

The fridge hums a tune so bright,
As we peek into the quiet night.
Neighbors argue, then break for snacks,
While walls chuckle at their little quacks.

A chair creaks, an old friend's joke,
As light switches flicker, then provoke.
Each echo holds a clue so neat,
Stories stuck beneath our feet.

Oh, the laughter trapped in seams,
As if the world were made of dreams.
Silly secrets the walls confide,
Ready for a joyful ride!

The Sound of Forgotten Dreams

Old ghosts tap-dance with delight,
Forgotten hopes take flight at night.
With silly hats and mismatched shoes,
They poke at us to share our views.

A clock ticks softly, breaks the norm,
While echoes of laughter weave and form.
The couch sighs, it knows our past,
With every giggle that it casts.

Beneath the bed, a sock brigade,
Hatches plans in a sock parade.
Dusting off the dreams we've kept,
In playful murmurs, they have leapt.

From curtains swaying, tales emerge,
Of silly blunders and a surge.
Each pulse of sound a playful tease,
Tickling the air like a light breeze.

Beneath the Layered Silence

Underneath the paint and grime,
A world of giggles, lost in time.
Cracks in walls hold secrets tight,
As they overhear our delight.

The ceiling's grin can't be contained,
It sways and brightens while it's strained.
Corners giggle, shadows play,
Telling tales in their own way.

With vibrant sighs, the old wood beams,
Share silly truths and quirky dreams.
Echoing chatter, with laughter plied,
In this stillness, they confide.

Jars filled with whispers, stored on shelves,
Show how we clumsily find ourselves.
Between the layers, joys reside,
In the stillness, side by side.

Underneath the Paint

Beneath the color, stories creep,
Of clumsy falls and laughter deep.
Every brush stroke hides an event,
As paint drips down, the time is spent.

The walls squabble 'bout worn-out jokes,
While cabinets share tales of quirky folks.
Old bottles rattle, tricks up their sleeves,
As the sunlight dances and weaves.

A door creaks low, a trusty mate,
Brings echoes of fun we can't negate.
Each smudge a memory, clearly laid,
In the corners where the laughter played.

So here's to the joy that paint can hide,
The silly moments stacked like a tide.
With every layer, smiles imbue,
In a colorful world, we all can view.

Bones of the Building Speak

In the attic, pipes do chatter,
Old wood groans, like a playful matter.
Windows rattle with all their might,
Chasing dust motes, in flickering light.

The floorboards creak, a comical dance,
Telling tales with a silly prance.
Creaking laughter fills the air,
As if those beams have stories to share.

Nails click together, a mid-night band,
The ceiling grumbles, as if it planned.
Each corner holds a giddy grin,
Promises of mischief deep within.

Who knew that bricks could crack a joke?
As laughter dances through the smoke.
Draperies shake, enjoying the jest,
In a home where humor never rests.

Secrets Interlaced with Silence.

In the corners, giggles hide,
Beneath the floor, they softly glide.
Drapes flutter like they're having fun,
As laughter bubbles, like a running gun.

A couch releases its tiny snore,
While a lamp winks, and offers more.
Together they plot a little prank,
On unsuspecting guests at the bank.

Sinks gurgle tunes of the past,
Rolling in rhythm, a sound so vast.
A mischievous cat chimes in quite well,
As secrets unfurl, laughter does swell.

In the stillness, the air does tease,
With chuckles contained in gentle breeze.
The amusing tales of a quiet night,
Keeping the peace in their delight.

Echoes in the Shadows

Soft echoes sing in the midnight gloom,
As shadows dance in an empty room.
A chair wobbles, it's got a plan,
To join the laughter, if it can.

The fridge hums secrets, juicy and rife,
Gossiping about late-night life.
While curtains sway like a ghostly laugh,
Sharing the tales of the aftermath.

A rug spins tales of footsteps near,
As toys chuckle, when humans feel fear.
Every crevice an insider's delight,
In a symphony of silliness, oh what a night!

The chandelier sways, keeping time,
With each chuckle, a sprightly rhyme.
In the dark, the quiet holds sway,
While mischief lurks in a playful way.

Secrets Beneath the Surface

Beneath the tiles, a tale starts to brew,
With giggles that bounce, in odd form or hue.
A grumpy old heater can't keep it in,
As laughter erupts, where chaos begins.

The plumbing pipes, all tangled and wise,
Trade jokes like letters, a clever disguise.
Bathtubs bubble like they're in a race,
In a splashy contest of pickles and grace.

Ducts that swoosh, tease magic in air,
Whirling their secrets without a care.
The walls grin wide, as night starts to fall,
Sharing their wisdom, a comical call.

A home brims with laughter, hidden so well,
As shadows gather and softly swell.
In every nook, full of playful jest,
Lives the heartbeat of fun, at its best.

Chords of the Invisible Choir

In the kitchen, pots clink loud,
The cat dances, feeling proud.
A spoon plays a joyful tune,
Like a mouse on the edge of June.

Beneath the sofa, socks conspire,
To catch the warmth of the fire.
Chairs creak as if they know,
All the secrets that we sow.

Lamps hum soft, a bright refrain,
Each flicker's like a friendly gain.
The fridge sings a midnight song,
"Snack time's where you all belong!"

In each corner, laughter grows,
With every slight, the mischief flows.
Voices jitter in the air,
Telling tales, beyond compare.

Realms of Reticent Rapture

Behind the door, a giggle hides,
As the dog in circles glides.
Basking in the glow of day,
He thinks he's won the grand ballet.

Cushions conspire, a soft parade,
As cats plot tricks that never fade.
Mice with capes live in delight,
While shadows dance on walls at night.

Teacups grin as tea is spilled,
Every droplet, joy-filled.
The curtains sway, they twist and twine,
In the room where secrets dine.

A clock laughs, its hands play tag,
With every tick, the memories brag.
You think it's still, but just you wait,
Time is quite the playful mate.

Past Lives in the Fabric

Stitched in seams, old tales live,
Fancy threads that never give.
Each patch a story, bold and bright,
Of sock puppets in a silly fight.

Grandma's quilt is a silent sage,
With every square, a funny page.
Something's hiding in the fold,
Tales of a sheep who loves the cold.

The couch, a ship on river dreams,
Navigating laughter's gleams.
Remote controls, they plot and scheme,
As popcorn kernels dance and gleam.

In every fabric, giggles roam,
Creating mischief in our home.
The ghost of fun will never fade,
In textures where the joy is laid.

Veils of Distant Echoes

Noisy echoes tiptoe near,
As laughter whispers 'over here!'
The walls are giggling out of turn,
While shadows twist, and candles burn.

Underneath, a mouse's dream,
Sketching plans with buttercream.
Each cupboard creaks with witty flair,
As countless crumbs fill up the air.

Beneath the stars, the night is wild,
A ruckus drawn, a playful child.
With knock-knock jokes from the attic space,
Even the night can't hide its face.

In every corner, joy can thrive,
As echoes hum, alive, alive!
The walls contain a jolly glee,
In a world that's always free.

Voices Hidden in the Hallways

In shadows dance a jester's glee,
A giggle floats behind a tree.
The echo of a secret tease,
Bouncing off the floor with ease.

A mouse in slippers, what a sight,
The cat just blinks, surprised at night.
They share a laugh, then scamper fast,
While sleepy folks forget the past.

The walls are thick with tales to tell,
Of mischief made, beneath the shell.
A ghost with puns, a specter spry,
Who cracks a joke, then fades nearby.

A laugh rings out from door to door,
The antics keep us wanting more.
In every nook, a chuckle sounds,
Where silly secrets know no bounds.

Reverberations of Forgotten Dreams

A sock without its rightful pair,
Claims it danced in midnight air.
A saucer spins, a cup takes flight,
As dreams collide in silly night.

A ghost who hums a lullaby,
With off-key notes that make us sigh.
The echoes clash, the giggles swell,
In every corner, tales compel.

An old broom sticks up for a dance,
While cookie crumbs take every chance.
The sleepy cat twirls like a king,
Around the room, they start to sing.

In corners dark, the fun ignites,
As shadows play on paper kites.
With every flash of laughter shared,
The night becomes a stage unprepared.

Unspoken Stories of the Night

The toaster moans, a sleepy tune,
While midnight snacks hold a big swoon.
The fridge hums softly, a tale in ice,
Where leftovers plot their paradise.

A chair that squeaks, it tells a score,
Of how it held a weighty bore.
But now it rocks with zest and zest,
In dreams of grandeur, it won't rest.

A lightbulb flickers, what a tease,
With secret thoughts that aim to please.
It flashes bright, then dims again,
Like laughter caught in a flow of rain.

In hidden nooks the stories roll,
From ceiling beams to dancing souls.
Each creak and crack a wink and grin,
Ensuring fun will always grin.

Hushed Tales in the Dark

The night is thick with muffled cheer,
As candlesticks start to reappear.
A whisper floats on playful breeze,
Of silly things behind the keys.

A cupboard creaks, a pot's awake,
They conspire over which to bake.
Flour dust fills the air with fun,
As kitchen chaos just begun.

The clock ticks slow, a wink it shares,
With every tick, it plays affairs.
So funny how the silence hums,
As finally everyone becomes.

Behind the door, a laughter rolls,
With bouncing notes from hidden souls.
In quiet corners of delight,
The magic stirs to gleeful heights.

Conversations with the Unseen

In the night, shadows sway,
Cracking jokes in a spooky way.
They tickle the air, causing a grin,
Is that a laugh from the closet within?

Ghostly chuckles in the hall,
Is it my mind or a pranking small?
Tales of socks lost to the void,
Did the cats laugh, or just feel annoyed?

Dust bunnies dance on the floor,
They open a dialogue, and I want more.
With a creak, the chair nods,
Is it polite, or just odd odds?

In the kitchen, pots clang with glee,
They're cooking up some ghostly tea.
"Sugar or salt?" I shout in delight,
They answer back, "Just don't take a bite!"

Secrets Carved in Timber

The old wood speaks, oh what a tale,
About a cat that had tried to sail.
Each creak, a giggle, a pun untold,
A diary of antics, daring and bold.

Floorboards moan like an old friend,
Whispering secrets that never end.
"Did you hear that?" I ask in jest,
No answer but laughter, forever blessed.

Chairs plot to spin when I'm not near,
Gossiping softly, but who do they fear?
Furniture meetings in the dim-lit den,
Planning their pranks like mischievous men.

As I settle down for the night,
I hear wood chuckling, it's quite a sight.
Sleepy woodheads, a party so bright,
In the heart of the house, still laughing tonight.

The Melodies of Ghostly Walls

In the hallway, echoes chime,
As walls hum tunes, a ghostly rhyme.
They sing of socks finding their match,
Of dusty secrets that always scratch.

Laughter bounces off plastered beams,
Hilarious tales, or so it seems.
A comedy club hosted by spooks,
Their punchlines shaped like old wooden nooks.

Windows giggle with every breeze,
The curtains flutter, a tease with ease.
"Join our show!" they beckon me near,
What's the punchline? I can barely hear!

As dawn breaks, the laughs recede,
But those ghostly melodies plant a seed.
For in every corner, a joke might lay,
Hiding in shadows, just waiting to play.

Dialogues in the Dark

When the lights dim and silence falls,
You can hear the chatter of ghostly calls.
"Did you see that?" one spirit says,
"No, but I felt it," another obeys.

A meeting of memories, untamed and free,
Discussing their past with great glee.
"Remember the time I knocked over a shoe?"
"Oh yes, dear ghost, how we all flew!"

The clock strikes twelve with a playful chime,
Ghostly laughter messes with time.
"Who's on next for the midnight show?"
"No one, but here comes the cat, quick, let's go!"

In the hush of the night, antics abound,
With uproarious debates, our ghosts are profound.
From shadow to shadow, they sashay with cheer,
In this silliness, there's naught left to fear!

Secrets in the Silence

In the corner, a giggle hides,
A secret that the cat decides.
Beans in a jar, a clatter, a fight,
As mice dance by in the pale moonlight.

Under the floor, a tale unfolds,
Of socks and treasures, stories bold.
The old clock sneezes, what's that about?
Tickle, tickle, then a loud shout!

Lurking behind the sturdy frame,
Is a fish named Fred who plays a game.
He splashes water, sends a spray,
While telling jokes in a watery way.

What's that sound? A dish takes flight,
As grandma yells, "Oh, not tonight!"
A ruckus reigns in this silly house,
With laughter echoing, even the mouse!

Sotto Voce of the Ages

In the attic, dust bunnies prance,
Their little dance makes ghosts take a chance.
With every shuffle, they giggle with glee,
As they plot a party, just wait and see!

The echoes of yesteryear tap on the floor,
With whispers of mischief, we ask for more.
Grandpa's old shoes, how they do jive,
Waltzing together, keeping dreams alive.

The old chair creaks, it tells a tale,
Of a cat named Bingo, and dogs on the trail.
They raced through the halls, a wild dog chase,
And tripped over shoes in a lively race!

Up on the shelf, old mugs confide,
Stories of coffee spills, they can't hide.
"Who made that mess?" they laugh in delight,
While we sip our tea, all cozy at night.

Cadences Lost in Time

Beneath the stairs, where shadows play,
A polka dot frog hops all day.
Croaking out tunes, a polka so fine,
With a splash in the pond, he'll take you to dine.

The wind chimes gossip, they jingle and sway,
Trading sweet secrets in an airy ballet.
While squirrels critique the poet's new verse,
With clever remarks, they may well rehearse.

A picture on the wall starts to wink,
As a sleepy old owl begins to think.
He hoots about parties from long ago,
When the moon was bright, and the stars all aglow.

In the hallway, a hiccup from the dog,
Who dreams of chasing around a fog.
He barks at the curtains, thinking they're friends,
While giggly giggles go on without ends.

Shades of Forgotten Lullabies

The couch is a ship with pillows for sails,
Captain Cat, with eye patches and tails.
He steers with paws through waves of the night,
While the goldfish watch from their bowl in delight.

Under the bed, a snack stash hides,
With crumbs telling stories, where wonder resides.
A snail named Larry joins for a feast,
While arguing fiercely on who's the least!

Chairs rock and sway, they're part of the crew,
As a sock puppet sails the great ocean blue.
With giggles abound and winks shared with glee,
They sail off to places beyond you and me.

When slumber comes softly, the night hums low,
Creatures and couches bask in the glow.
In this comical world, laughter calls each night,
While dreams are sailing, 'neath stars shining bright.

Writings on the Wall

In the bathroom, notes hang tight,
A grocery list in fading light.
Tomatoes, pickles, and a shoe,
Seems someone's hungry for a stew!

Behind the door, a joke finds home,
'Why did the chicken? Just to roam!'
Laughter echoes, silly and free,
Who left this comedy for me?

On the kitchen tiles, secrets sprawled,
'Left your lunch? The fridge was called!'
A peanut butter love affair,
With jelly jealous, oh beware!

Yet in this space, where echoes play,
The walls have tales in their own way.
From post-it notes to silly scrawls,
Life's a jest behind these walls!

Poetry from Shadows

In dusk's embrace, shadows align,
A sock debates, 'You're almost mine!'
Is that a shoe? Or just a ghost?
These pairings are what matter most.

A cat thinks it's the wall's best friend,
She bats at shapes that twist and bend.
'You think you're clever?' she seems to say,
'Caught you laughing at me today!'

In corners dark, a broom does waltz,
'To clean or not, that's my faults!'
Dust bunnies dance in the moon's glow,
Finding tricks we'll never know.

There's humor here in dumb debates,
In painted bricks and creaky slates.
The laughter blends with night's parade,
With every shadow game they played.

Quietude in Crumbling Edges

Along the cracks, a tale does hum,
Pencil vases and a used gum.
'This is where my wisdom lies,'
Said the wall, adorned in lies.

A splatter here, a dribble there,
Tales of snacks and wild repair.
Each chipped edge holds a story,
Of cats and dogs and minor glory.

The attic hold's a treasure chest,
A squirrel's pantry, it's no jest!
Snacks untouched, yet dreams remain,
Of nutty treats and joyful rain.

In quietude, the humor throngs,
Echoing in forgotten songs.
For in these edges, life does bloom,
With giggles in the dust and gloom.

The Soft Footfall of History

Old shoes linger in corners still,
They often dance with ghostly thrill.
'Tap your heels, and let's have fun,'
Said history, 'The night's not done.'

In these chambers, stories prance,
From fancy balls to silly dance.
'Step on in!' the echoes shout,
Join the fun, there's no doubt!

With every creak of weary wood,
Laughter stirs where silence stood.
A tale of socks and haughty shoes,
In herstory's ball, we'll never lose.

So here's to steps, both quick and slow,
Echoes of jest where time won't go.
For every footfall, there's a song,
And history hums where we belong.

Murmurs in the Midnight Hour

In the stillness, a gentle snore,
A cat sings low, what a silly roar!
The fridge hums tunes of old rock bands,
While shadows dance, forming silly strands.

A sock's escape from the laundry pile,
Discussing dreams in a cat-like style.
The clock ticks gossip of times gone by,
While dust bunnies plot, oh my oh my!

The creaky door shares secrets untold,
Of midnight snacks and the world's cold gold.
A slipper whispers of a race gone wrong,
While laughter echoes like a silly song.

In this symphony of nighttime play,
Each object joins in, hip-hip-hooray!
A chorus of giggles, a friendly brawl,
Oh, the great tales spun by night's soft call.

Silent Conversations

In the corner, the chair has a chat,
With the curtain, who's dressed like a cat.
They giggle about the dust that rained,
And the covert crumbs that remain untrained.

The teapot chimes in, with a dented sigh,
While the dustpan argues, "Oh, tell me why?"
The kettle's hot laugh bubbles in cheer,
Toasting the night and all who are near.

A potato's tale of being mashed,
Is met with a grumble from a fork well-hashed.
The bread loaf loiters, a bit on the sly,
With tales of the toaster, "I knew him, oh my!"

Through these unspoken, funny views,
Lie tales of mishaps and silly blues.
Who knew a kitchen could laugh so loud?
With every utensil, funny and proud.

Hidden Voices Unbound

In the attic, a suitcase claps its lid,
Telling secrets of places it hid.
The light bulb flickers, sharing a joke,
Lighting up memories, like an old smoke.

The broomstick chuckles at the dust it sweeps,
While old toys gossip while no one peeps.
A teddy bear snickers, a bit worn-out,
As it reminisces about a boy's clout.

The old gramophone plays tunes of yore,
While a mouse taps toes, begging for more.
Each forgotten corner hums with delight,
As objects spin stories deep into the night.

What's this? The wallpaper gives a sigh,
Recalling tales of a winking eye.
In this hideaway, voices break free,
Sharing laughs that only the night can see.

Soft Utterances of Old

In the study, a chair speaks of rest,
Planned lazy afternoons, truly the best.
The bookshelf chuckles, stocked with some puns,
As papers dance in the light of the sun.

Old slippers gossip while they wait by the door,
About travels and walks, and oh, so much more!
The mantel clock giggles at time slipping by,
Chiming in laughter, oh, my my my!

An old stereo started to croon,
About dances gone by to a sleepy tune.
The coffee pot grumbles, "Where's my brew?"
Sharing tales of mornings with laughter anew.

Cozy blankets whisper 'let's take a nap,'
While the couch joins in, "I'll wrap you, that's that!"
In this haven of chatter, soft and bold,
Lie comedies shared, in utterances old.

The Echo Chamber of Memory

In a room where jokes collide,
Echoes dance, they cannot hide.
Silly thoughts, like bouncing balls,
Giggling loud in shadowed halls.

Memories dressed in mismatched shoes,
Tickling toes, giving a bruise.
Laughter leaks from every seam,
What a wild, wonderful dream!

Walls are gossiping, so absurd,
With every giggle, a jumbled word.
In this chamber of antics bright,
Daydreams wink in sheer delight.

Time drifts on, a merry kite,
Juggling sights, both odd and light.
The past, it dances with a grin,
A joyful party tucked within.

Whispers of Yesterday

A cat that talks with a sassy tone,
Recalls the days when we sat alone.
Chasing tails and purring loud,
Crafty tales of the kitchen crowd.

The toaster hums a zany tune,
Of burnt bread under a silver moon.
Silly secrets it likes to share,
Of breakfast shenanigans and morning flair.

Lampshades shake in raucous joy,
As dust bunnies play with a toy.
In every corner, a giggle grows,
Painting smiles where no one goes.

Yesterday's mischief, today's delight,
Echoes twirling in the soft twilight.
With a wink, the past takes a bow,
In the theater of laughter, here and now.

Unspoken Words in the Quiet

In corners where the secrets hum,
Ticklish thoughts begin to come.
An old chair creaks with tales so grand,
Of silly pranks and bands unplanned.

The fridge is filled with whispered dreams,
Of pie fights and chocolate screams.
Invisible jokes fly in the air,
Like jellybeans tossed without a care.

Underneath the bed, a rumor spreads,
Of mismatched socks and sleepy heads.
Tangled stories, a playful tease,
Floating like laughter through the breeze.

A hat that dances with a flair,
Each fold contains a secret rare.
In silence, craziness takes a stroll,
Silent giggles define the whole.

Murmurs Beyond the Gloom

In the depths of a shadowy nook,
Silly sounds come with a look.
Crickets chirp in rhythm's play,
Singing nonsense till break of day.

The old clock chuckles with every tick,
Counting moments both odd and quick.
Ghostly pranks from yesterday's crew,
Telling tales of the things they'd do.

Curtains sway in laughter's embrace,
As shadows leap and frolic in space.
The floorboards hum a joking tune,
Beneath the glow of the silver moon.

Echoes play, from dark to light,
Dancing mischief in the night.
Through gloom and giggles, joy will bloom,
Spirits rise beyond the gloom.

The Soundscape of Solace

In the hallway, a squeaky shoe,
Bouncing echoes like a playful crew.
A cat's meow mimics a cartoon chase,
As the neighbor's frog joins the race.

Pots and pans create a band,
While a toddler conducts with a snack in hand.
Chairs creak like an old-timey tune,
Creating laughter 'neath the bright full moon.

Distant chuckles through the air,
As the dog barks without a care.
An unseen party surely sways,
In harmony of comical ways.

Quiet Observations of the Unseen

Behind the curtain, a tickle of glee,
As the old man waves to the neighbor's tree.
Noses peek out from the blinds in surprise,
While a squirrel juggles acorns, oh what a prize!

The TV hums with sitcoms and cheers,
A baby giggles, waving bye to fears.
Laughter echoes like it's on repeat,
As ghosts join in for a dance on their feet.

Paper rustles as secrets unfold,
A cat plays hide-and-seek, bold and uncontrolled.
Invisible pals share a silly spree,
In this carnival of joy, wild and free.

Conductors of the Invisible

A clatter and pitter, the counters debate,
As spoons conduct a symphonic fate.
Chairs squeak with wisdom, low and wise,
While a shadow pirouettes, to surprise!

The floor creaks gossip of friendship so dear,
As the toaster pops, lending a cheer.
An unseen maestro, orchestrating it all,
While mischief thrives in every hall.

Laughter bubbles like boiling stew,
As jigsaw puzzles form a crew.
Each tick and tock, a giggle from time,
Joining forces in a rhythm sublime.

Sonic Threads of Connection

Beneath the stairs, a chuckle takes flight,
As socks roam boldly into the night.
Scurrying mice in tap shoed delight,
A symphony of silliness, pure as light.

An ice cream truck plays a ghostly song,
While two goldfish gossip all day long.
The fridge hums a tune of secrets so sweet,
As the broom taps a beat, oh what a feat!

Echoes of giggles, a thrilling resound,
Spinning tales in a merry-go-round.
Invisible threads weave the cheer,
In a merry dance far and near.

Subterranean Stories

In the cellar where the shadows play,
Ghosts recount tales in a jolly way.
With pickled jars and old shoes stacked,
They laugh at every secret pact.

A cat named Mittens guards the door,
He swears he's heard a ghostly snore.
But really it's just Aunt Mabel's pies,
She bakes them late, oh how time flies!

Underneath the floorboards' creaky creaks,
A family of mice share all their leaks.
They gossip about the sugar stored,
And dream of the cake they can't afford!

With every thud and bump from above,
They chuckle and dance, oh the fun they love.
In this strange realm where tales combine,
Even the dust has stories divine!

The Tune of Timelessness

In the attic, a radio plays so loud,
Tunes of old dance and make the dust proud.
The ghost of Grandpa taps his foot,
With a style that's quite a hoot!

A broomstick band joins in the song,
While a squirrel plays a chirpy gong.
The shadows twist and swirl around,
In this jolly jam, fun is found!

Clocks tick tock without a care,
Time's pranks are hidden everywhere.
A minute spent could be a year,
Or it disappears—oh my, how queer!

Yet laughter rings, an endless reel,
Even time can't keep this zeal.
So join the tune of timeless cheer,
As jokes and giggles fill the sphere!

Lingering Melodrama

A doorway creaks, what's that I hear?
Sounds like a soap opera's premier!
With curtains drawn, the drama shows,
As spatulas duel in kitchen prose.

A fight over cake becomes quite a scene,
Who took the last slice? It's a mystery keen!
The fridge is the judge, so cold and wise,
With ice cubes ready to serve up surprise!

In corners of rooms, the arguments bloom,
As shadows bicker and spell out doom.
But wait, what's that? A giggle, a charm,
Turns quarrels to laughter, it's quite disarm!

These walls have tales of squabbles and fun,
Where even the curtains join in the run.
With a flip and a flap, the audience sways,
As laughter and spatulas steal the days!

A Symphony of Shadows

In the night, shadows leap and bound,
Creating a symphony, what a sight!
A chair plays the drums, steady and round,
While the cupboard hums with pure delight.

The windows tinkle with gentle laughter,
As moonlight dances upon the floor.
Each flicker and twist leads to big fun after,
With every creak echoing tales galore!

A sock on the mantle takes center stage,
Performing a tango, a sight to behold!
While the broom joins in with a rhythmic rage,
All the laughter outside turns to gold!

In this waltz of the night, all fear takes flight,
As giggles rise high and spirits soar.
In shadowy corners, pure joy shines bright,
A symphony of silliness forevermore!

Sounds of Forgotten Places

In dusty corners, secrets reside,
A creaky chair makes quite the guide.
The cat meows like it's telling jokes,
While old wood floors sing of sleeping folks.

A tick-tock buddy plays hide and seek,
While echoes of laughter sneak and squeak.
Bumbled thoughts like socks left behind,
In the attic, a treasure hard to find.

Kettle sings a tune on a lazy day,
While grumpy clocks tick by in dismay.
The fridge hums tales of meals long past,
As we chuckle at our shadows cast.

In hidden nooks, memories collide,
Where silly sounds and giggles abide.
Each wall holds a story, vibrant and spry,
Of times that made us laugh till we cry.

Unvoiced Memories in Stillness

Beneath the stairs, a ghost plays charades,
Cereal bowls dance in their own parades.
A sock jumps out, refusing to dwell,
On the lost laundry tales it could tell.

Tupperware lids play musical chairs,
While the refrigerator hatches zany affairs.
Old shoes giggle, longing for a stroll,
As chatter erupts from a forgotten bowl.

The couch grumbles with a comfy sigh,
Dreaming of snacks it could supply.
A friendly ghost, in poltergeist glee,
Quips, "Ever tried tickling your TV?"

In corners where silence dares to creep,
Are tales that make the heart take a leap.
With every creak, let laughter restore,
The stories of a house, forever more.

Faint Hum of Antiquity

An old rocking chair creaks with delight,
Telling tales of cozy, long-gone nights.
Pots hum softly, busy with stews,
As if they're sharing long-lost news.

Grandpa's clock winks as he counts the fun,
While dust motes dance in warm rays of sun.
In antiquated whispers, mischief is cast,
As items wonder if they'll be outlasted.

A lamp flickers, flicking funny puns,
While old photos giggle—oh, aren't we fun?
A cupboard chuckles, hiding its prize,
A half-eaten cookie that never says goodbye.

In the quiet, laughter echoes so sweet,
As history's clutter can't be beat.
Each subtle sound tells a story well-worn,
Of moments shared and memories reborn.

Eloquent Silence

The clock whispers with a tick-tock grin,
While the sofa holds secrets just within.
In a still room, laughter lingers like air,
Secrets shared in a way that's rare.

An empty chair seems to nod and sway,
Welcoming jokes in a playful way.
A book opens wide, with pages aglow,
Sharing wisdom only dogs seem to know.

Creaky shutters gossip about the breeze,
Tickling the silken curtains with ease.
A floorboard chuckles with every second,
As it recalls the times it reckoned.

In elegant quiet, the walls catch it all,
The giggles, the secrets, the memories small.
Let's toast to the silence that dances and calls,
Creating our laughter within these old walls.

The Whispered Histories

In shadows, secrets dance and play,
Old tales snicker, never gray.
Dusty portraits wiggle their brows,
While cobwebs giggle beneath their vows.

Squeaky floorboards share a joke,
As a picture frame begins to choke.
With every creak, a chuckle grows,
The house itself knows all the lows.

Chairs that rock, with glee they shake,
And curtains flap, for laughter's sake.
A teapot whirls, spills tea on floor,
As ghosts retell what came before.

Fossilized footprints of a cat,
Strolling through tales, fancy that!
With every crack, the nostalgia swells,
In the lively chatter of hidden bells.

Chronicles of the Unseen

Behind the paint, a giggle hides,
Where laughter loops like wild rides.
An old clock winks, time plays along,
Tick-tocking out a silly song.

The pipes gurgle a comic spree,
As mice scuttle, making glee.
Behind the walls, a madcap crew,
Pretend to host a grand debut.

A hint of mischief fills the air,
With echoes of a jester's flair.
Stickers stuck on the back of dreams,
Crafting laughter in moonlit beams.

Every corner holds a grin,
As stories tumble, tumble in.
So pour a drink, lift your chin,
For madness thrives where tales begin.

Scratches in the Silence

In the quiet, scratches glide,
Little paws that scoot and hide.
A lizard's tail flicks tales untold,
While shadows gather, young and old.

A riddle echoes, what's wrong or right?
Walls chuckle deep into the night.
An old sock dances, throws a fit,
As laughter erupts, can't quit, can't quit.

Door knobs jiggle with a prankish glee,
All the while, we sip our tea.
The fridge hums jokes of past regrets,
Grinning at all of life's frets.

So join the fun, come take a glance,
At what your walls might dare to dance.
For in the quiet, once in a while,
You'll find the absurd hides with a smile.

Veiled Voices Amidst Dust

Amidst the dust, the whispers swirl,
Tiny voices twist and unfurl.
A chandelier does a little shimmy,
As curtains sway, oh so whimsy.

In corners, clinks and clanks abound,
Where the mischief and humor are found.
Old shoes shuffle, no need for feet,
While echoes join in with the beat.

A broomstick taps with rhythm divine,
Declaring to bowls that it's time to dine.
Dust bunnies giggle, taking a stand,
In a world where nonsense is grand.

Here secrets laugh, and jokes ignite,
In the soft glow of the waning light.
So come, fellow traveler, hear the fun,
In a home where the laughter won't run.

Echoes of Silent Murmurs

In the quiet of the night, a sock jumps high,
Invisible clowns dance, oh my oh my!
The fridge hums a tune, a delightful mess,
Telling secrets of snacks, as it tries to impress.

The cat sits and stares with a baffled look,
Wondering why the chair is a favorite nook.
As spoons and forks jive on the kitchen floor,
A party for one, who's keeping the score?

Loud whispers of slippers on the wooden ground,
Silly ghosts giggling in a playful sound.
Tick-tock goes the clock, it's a comedy show,
Where the walls hold their breath in delightful glow.

They laugh at the creaks, a hilarious tune,
Two ghosts do the tango, bright as the moon.
Each chuckle and sigh, a joke they could tell,
In the comical chorus where the shadows dwell.

Secrets Beneath the Surface

Underneath the sink, there's a secret lair,
Where old spoons gather for a wild affair.
They talk about times when they stirred the pot,
And argue whose turn it is, it's all they've got.

Behind closed doors, a rubber band sings,
Dreaming of days when it could wear wings.
While tupperware grumbles about its tight lid,
Claiming its absence has always been hid.

The TV hums softly, sharing its woes,
While the couch cushions plot how to steal the show.
They giggle and whisper of sitcom delights,
Crafting new scripts for their weekly sights.

In the pile of laundry, a sock snickers loud,
Sharing stories of tumble from a spinning crowd.
Together they tease about missing mates,
As secrets unfold from their cozy states.

Conversations in the Shadows

In the dim-lit corners where shadows collide,
A broom and a vacuum share secrets with pride.
They gossip about crumbs that try to escape,
While dust bunnies giggle, forming a shape.

A lamp takes a breather, its light feels confused,
Joking about times it was utterly used.
The book on the shelf talks of wild fantasy,
While its page-turner buddy follows with glee.

The coat rack makes quips about jackets and hats,
Competing for space with hosting acrobats.
Each hanging garment has a story to share,
Of travel adventures, they can hardly bear.

With each little creak, a wisecrack resounds,
Furniture laughs as they spin 'round in bounds.
In a world of the brave, these shadows convene,
They create a hilarity, silently seen.

Subtle Sounds of Solitude

In the corner of the room, a pencil's drawn,
Sketching out dreams till the very dawn.
The coffee pot bubbles with a cheeky grin,
Sharing gossip of brews and where they've been.

A chair squeaks with laughter, a playful slide,
Challenging the table to another ride.
With every tick of a clock, the jokes unfold,
The tales of time passing, both silly and bold.

A tear in the fabric, it chuckles and sighs,
Complaining of those who pass by, oh my!
While the window considers a breeze like a tease,
Spreading tales of outside, with much flair to please.

The floorboards attempt to join in the fun,
Bouncing with rhythm as if they could run.
In the calm of the evening, a quirky ballet,
They dance and they chat until the end of the day.

Ghostly Breaths of Abandon

In the attic where the old socks hide,
A ghost urges me to take a ride.
He laughs as he points to an empty chair,
I swear it's not just the stale air!

Newspapers flutter with secrets to share,
Their headlines tickle and fill me with flair.
A bat swoops down, a friend in disguise,
We dance through cobwebs and tell silly lies!

The clock strikes twelve, it's time for a game,
The ghosts compete in a race for fame.
Such playful spirits, they never interfere,
Just giggles and pranks, oh so sincere!

With every chuckle, the shadows grow bright,
We toast with cold tea to the brands of fright.
In the funhouse echoes, we revel and play,
In this haunted story, we'll never stray!

The Softest Sighs of Time

Tick-tock, the old clock makes a sound,
A turtle's pace, it's quite renowned.
It sneezes a feather, all dust and glee,
I swear it winked; was it just me?

In the corner, a chair starts a snore,
The rug laughs loud, it can't take anymore.
An old book giggles as it turns a page,
Echoing tales of a wise, ancient sage.

Laughter bubbles from beneath the floor,
A mouse in a cap knows the latest lore.
He tells of a party in a shoe,
With popcorn confetti and drinks made of dew!

While I sit and ponder this wonderful place,
Time tickles my ear with a gentle embrace.
Funny stories linger, soft as a chime,
In this quirky abode, where nothing's a crime!

Fleeting Notes on the Breeze

A breeze flutters by with a chuckle profound,
It carries old tunes from the ground all around.
The daffodils hum in a vibrant chat,
While squirrels debate who's the finest acrobat.

Feathered friends chirp, a new tune to play,
As wind becomes laughter, night turns to day.
A dandelion puffs out a giggly surprise,
Floating off gently, like playful butterflies.

The trees shake their leaves, a comedic dance,
Twirling and swirling, they take every chance.
A chipmunk in shades thinks it's all quite grand,
While the sun giggles down, a fiery band.

Nature's a jester, with joy that's contagious,
Every little moment is simply outrageous.
As the breeze whispers laughter, I can't help but tease,
In this world of nonsense, I'm eager to please!

Unseen Dialogues of Dust

The dust bunnies gather for a secret affair,
Discussing their plans while hiding in hair.
They tell jokes about socks that have lost their mates,
Creating a ruckus that simply elates.

Each tumbleweed tumble knows a few puns,
Spinning tales of lost keys and runaway runs.
A quaint little selfie with a rogue dust mote,
Captures their charm, on a soap bubble boat.

Chairs creak in laughter, sharing their views,
The wallpaper's giggle adds colorful hues.
They're plotting a skit, with glitter and fun,
In this hidden world where wild pranks run.

At day's end, the dust settles in play,
As laughter lingers at the close of the day.
The unseen dialogues spin tales, it's true,
In corners of rooms where the magic shines through!

Tales the Walls Could Tell

If these bricks could share a tale,
They'd laugh at cats, their daily fail.
They'd overhear the softest sigh,
As sneezes dance and laughter fly.

A sock that vanished in the night,
Claimed by the couch, what a delight!
The bickering of spoons at play,
While forks just roll their eyes, ballet.

From midnight snacks to dance-off frights,
They witness it all, oh what sights!
Could walls delight in every quirk?
As noises within give them a smirk.

So raise a glass to what they know,
Hidden fun that's put on show.
For every crack, a giggle whole,
With every bump, a secret soul.

Voices Beneath the Plaster

In the corners, small voices scheme,
As dust bunnies plot their dream.
They gossip of shoes left behind,
While mice talk cheese, oh how they grind!

"Oh, look at this odd sock, so bright!"
Squeaked a mouse in the dead of night.
"Is that a shoe? Oh what a sight,
Perhaps we'll hold a style fight!"

The paint peels off, they watch with glee,
As the family fights over TV.
The walls can't help but snicker loud,
At clumsy falls that stir the crowd.

So if you listen close one day,
You'll hear the tales they like to play.
For even plaster has its fun,
In the home where laughter's spun.

Echoes from Yesterday

Oh, the echoes from times gone by,
Where grandma's laugh meets a shy cry.
The toddler's tantrum, a classic scene,
While walls just chuckle, "Oh, how keen!"

"Remember that time?" the wallpaper asks,
As wallpaper peels, revealing tasks.
"Oh yes, indeed!" says the old chair's creak,
"Funny how you once made me speak!"

The fridge groans low, a humor foul,
As leftovers plot a scent, a scowl.
"Is it lunch or last week's delight?"
The walls just giggle at the sight.

So let your laughter ride the breeze,
And give your worries a light tease.
For in these echoes, joy prevails,
In all the stories that humor tells.

Conversations of the Carrion

The old bones rattle, oh so spry,
As if to join the living sigh.
"I once could move!" one joins the jest,
While mice debate which cheese is best.

Their banter echoes through the night,
As shadows play in eerie light.
"A skeleton's dance is quite the show,"
Said the old book, a little slow.

"Don't forget the ghost with no shoes!"
Squeaked a mouse with a search for clues.
"His tragic state brings such great glee,
For who would haunt with bare, cold feet?"

So listen close to the odd affair,
The laughter lingers in the air.
Among the bones, a party thrives,
In spooky fun, the humor dives.

Songs of Echoing Existence

In the hall where echoes play,
A sock sings of laundry day.
The fridge hums a mellow tune,
While dishes plot to leave by noon.

A spoon clinks with a friendly cheer,
It swears it's the best chandelier.
The clock ticks with a cheeky grin,
Counting all the laughs within.

Beneath the stairs, a cat's soft purr,
Teases tales of a nightly blur.
The vacuum dances with a twirl,
As if it's got a secret girl.

Oh, the walls have secrets, oh so grand,
Of spilled cake and lost rubber bands.
In each creak, there lies a jest,
In the game of home, we're all the best.

Hidden Harmonies in the Ether

Behind the door, a sneeze takes flight,
A melody of pure delight.
When dishes clash, the spoons all croon,
A raucous tune at half-past noon.

The chair squeaks out a laugh, they say,
Whenever a bum takes a sway.
The cat's paw slips, a slapstick show,
While socks collide in a footwear throw.

A fridge giggles in hum and buzz,
As it recalls the last big fuzz.
Each drip from the tap a secret hum,
In the kitchen, it's always fun.

The walls chuckle with tales so sly,
Of how the last cupcake did die.
In every corner, a story's spun,
In this funny home, we're all but one.

Asynchronous Calls of the Unheard

In the quiet, the toilet sighs,
As it dreams of brighter skies.
The kettle cackles, bubbling with glee,
Echoes bouncing like a lively spree.

An umbrella with a secret grudge,
Skirts the puddles, refuses to budge.
Cushions mutter, lending their weight,
As the couch holds a sarcastic fate.

The toaster pops like a dirty joke,
While crumbs scatter, a happy smoke.
The doorbell rings, a text message sings,
As the floor plays games with shoes and strings.

Walls lean in, eager and keen,
To overhear what's never seen.
In this house, a comedy thrives,
With laughter as the spark that drives.

The Soft Palette of Sound

In the shadows, the curtains twitch,
Like they're trying to find a niche.
The lamp hums low, a warm embrace,
While the clock rolls its eyes in space.

Beneath the floorboards, giggles burst,
From the party that's unrehearsed.
Each creak and clack, a playful note,
This home sings as a reveling boat.

The blender whirls with giddy zest,
While the stirring spoon just won't rest.
Together they dance, a quirky choir,
Of spaghetti sauce, a wild desire.

The walls, they blush at the tales they keep,
Of midnight snacks and secrets deep.
In this orchestra of life, so spry,
Every corner holds a laugh-filled sigh.

www.ingramcontent.com/pod-product-compliance
Lightning Source LLC
Chambersburg PA
CBHW060131230426
43661CB00003B/380